POEMO ERECTUS

POEMO ERECTUS

CONTENTS

CONTENTS CONT.

ACKNOWLEDGEMENTS

First, I must thank my son's friend Geoffrey for shining his light into the darkness of my closet and assuring me it was okay to come out.

Secondly, I owe a debt of gratitude to my favorite Canadian crush, Zachary Wilde, whose Adonis-like beauty, and unabashed feistiness, had been a perpetual source of inspiration over the years that turned into many of the poems in this book.

Special thanks go to my young adult brain trust Brett Moore and Quinton Jack, who provided me with much needed unbiased criticisms and motivation.

I'm especially thankful for the very talented Nancy Ann of Nancy Ann B Photography and Graphic Design for working her magic and making the concept of this book become a reality.

INTRODUCTION

Homosexuality. Homosexual. Gay. Yes, I just wrote those words. In fact, I chose to begin the introduction to this book with those words because I believe there is nothing wrong or shameful about them. They are merely words useful in describing a person, like myself, with a same sex preference. And, I believe that there is nothing wrong, or shameful, about anyone these words may describe. These words have existed in cultures and civilizations of the world throughout history. And, why? You guessed it. Because people like me and you have always existed. There is clear evidence that homosexuality not only existed but was quite prevalent in Ancient Greece and within the Roman Empire. It is also known that homosexuality was much more accepted by both of those ancient societies.

The society I grew up in was not accepting of people who were, let's say, different. So, most people my age learned early on to conceal their true selves, wants, desires. They sacrificed self to fit in, to be and act normal and acceptable as society dictated. I went through my entire youth, teen years, on into young adulthood, never fully understanding why I had the greatest crushes on guys, why I had no interest in dating girls. I did my best to play along at being normal. Why, I even married (a woman) and had a family! I'm sure many of you reading this have experienced, or are experiencing, something similar in your lives. Let's be honest, the closet is a lonely place in which to live. It took well into adulthood for me to summon the courage to finally come out--first to myself, and then to the world. For those of you who may still be in the closet, I trust this book enlightens, as well as entertains, while passing the time waiting to hatch. But much more importantly, I hope in some small way it may inspire a Shaw Shank Redemption epiphany—your finally breaking out.

When I first broke out of sexual identity bondage, I moved to
Key West, Florida. It's been said that all roads lead to Rome.
Well, I'd also heard that for we different folk, all roads lead
to Key West--primarily because it reports having a large
gay population. I sought a safe place in which to become
myself, to try out my new wings, and to grow increasingly
more comfortable within my new skin. It was quite the
metamorphosis!

This collection of poems blossomed out of the period of
my own personal blossoming. They were inspired by people,
places, and things I encountered while on my new journey.
They represent a peek into my personal experiences, both good
and bad. I wrote many to vent, some to lament, and others in
celebration of those rare, but oh so sweet, victories. I wrote
and wrote and filed everything away to never be seen again by
human eyes. Recently, I realized how selfish that was. Perhaps
my poems, good or bad, might bring a smile, some laughter,
or a glimmer of hope to someone in need of a poke, a prod, a
spiritual uplifting.

It's been said that one does not light a candle and then place it
under a basket. The purpose of candlelight is to be shared. We,
too, each have a light within ourselves that we must become
less fearful about letting it shine. Be proud of who you are.
I'm proud. And, I'm proud to be a member of our extended
LGBTQ family of youngsters and oldsters alike.

Now, let us render unto Caesar that which is Caesar's, and
unto poetry that which is…well…why don't I just let you
decide.

Peace, love, and rainbow tho'ts,

~g

I

TEESUS

KISS

Close, coming closer,
gentle, heated
breath.

Mouth meeting mouth,
warm, soft lips
caress.

Tongue tasting tongue,
long, passionate
kiss.

~g

BETWEEN THE LINES

You say things
to me
so sensitive
and sweet
a straight boy
would never say,
with that smile
on his face,
and that twinkle
in his eyes.
All signs that
give you away.

~g

HUMAN CONUNDRUM
(Not to be confused with condom)

Why do we humans
seem to suck so bad
at being human?
Why do we seem
to run away from the
that we need most?

Why do we seem
to deny the truth
about our own
needs, wants,
desires, feelings,
sexuality,
not only to others,
but more shamefully,
to ourselves?

Why can't we simply
reach out and touch,
and let others
reach out and touch
back, when touch and
touching is what
we each crave most
in our lives?

Why do we seem
to harbor so much

fear when it comes
to sharing pleasure ~
fear of self, others,
guilt, failure,
disappointment,
disease, and
the greatest, most
hideous of all:
liking it, and being
labeled for it?

Heterosexual,
homosexual,
metrosexual,
why not simply
enjoy it as it was
meant to be enjoyed:
freely, fully,
with no labeling,
fear, or shame?

Could it simply be,
after all is said
and done,
that we humans
really do suck
at being human?

~g

DARE TO EXPLORE

Have you thumbed through
the myriad of magazines
scattered in piles
here and there
on the floor?

Have you carefully studied
the plethora of paintings
hanging on walls,
room to room,
door to door?

Have your fingers run over
the titles of books
crammed randomly
upon shelf,
after shelf?

For in exploring more
that which is me,
you'll more deeply
discover
yourself.

~g

PERFECT

Something has
become quite
clear.
You're someone
I love to have
near.
Should you ask
me why
I really like you,
guy,
it's because
you're
so perfectly
queer.

~g

SCHOOL OF DENIAL

I was smart, at the
head of my class.
Opportunities came.
I let them pass.

Lettered four years
in two hard sports,
held leadership
roles of all sorts.

Best dressed, most
likely to succeed,
the "go to boy"
for any need.

Edited and wrote
the school news,
popular as hell,
yet had the blues.

I felt an emptiness
deep inside. While
others had fun, I went
along for the ride.

Never dated and
didn't know why.
Girls just never did
it for this guy.

There wasn't any
Real World on TV,
nothing to teach me
how to be the real me.

~g

THE CRAYOLA PEOPLE

The colors of my world have
become so wonderfully new.
My old home a mean red,
me, somewhat green, and
my old life was so blue.

Like a chameleon, I tried
to make myself fit in:
sometimes yellow from fear
of things yet unknown about
the new life I longed to live.

Other times, green with envy
of those living that life,
who have always lived it,
the Crayola people: society's
misfits bound by love.

Green, yellow, or blue,
they warmly welcomed me.
Green, yellow, or blue,
they accepted me with a
great big orange hug.

In Crayola world, all colors
in the box are welcome.
In Crayola world, all colors
blend together into a
gentle, passionate purple.

~g

ACCEPTANCE

I'm not a friend you'd imagine,
or ever come to expect;
but one who'd always be there,
when others do neglect.

I'm called odd, a little different,
some may say I'm queer.
It shouldn't even matter much,
when motives are sincere.

A friend's a friend regardless if
his girlfriend's name is Ted.
There's so much more to others
than who they take to bed.

I'm a warm, sociable person,
not some social disease;
a slight aberration of Nature,
(ever slight, if you please.)

I've a big heart and joyful spirit,
as you have come to see,
a true-blue friend forever yours,
if you'd be the same to me.

~g

DAWN OF THE ORANGE PEOPLE

Under the cloak of darkness
they journey out of hiding
to a secret place that
welcomes them.
Tonight, they gather in the
greatest of numbers,
abandoning caution,
defying warnings of an
immense release of energy
and coming of color.

The joyful reunion unleashes
their deepest emotions,
hidden for so long out of
fear of persecution.
Suppressed passion rises
quickly and intensely,
until the night air quietly,
yet violently erupts into
bright, surging bursts
of orange.

The pulsating glow
penetrates the night sky,
lighting up the mountains,
valleys, and the great sea.
Today, the world awakens
long before sunrise to
a new kind of dawn,
of a people wanting only to
love freely, and openly, in
the brightest light of day.

~g

SUCH A RUSH

What is it about you?
I cannot explain
why I find myself
driven to stop
and take special
notice of you.

When the bus arrives,
I stand there
waiting,
watching,
looking for that first
glimpse of you.

In between classes,
I linger at my
locker risking
being late,
hoping to catch a
glance from you.

What is it about me?
I have a girlfriend.
Yet, when she's
with me, I cannot
keep my mind
off of you.

Christ, you're a guy!
What the fuck!
Am I losing it,
or just now
discovering my
true identity?

What is it about you
that I crave
so badly,
and in a way
I fear may never
be possible?

You're such a rush!

~g

MORE-MEN

Young, handsome,
conservative, and
devout Christian,
he lives in denial
on the right.

Despite his lifestyle
and strict morés,
he always feels
depressed and
so uptight.

Seems he feels
most happy when
he's all alone
in his
room at night,

In only a thong
and ear buds,
twerking his
bubble ass
with delight.

He longs to be a
club dancer, his
body sparkling
with glitter in
the limelight,

His thong stuffed
with dollar bills,
the other boys
ignoring him
out of spite.

A latent, liberal,
Adonis, freeing
his captive spirit
from its closeted
prison at night.

~g

CARDINAL SIN

A beautiful young boy
with plumage of red,
perches upon a rock
by the riverbed.

I watch, sipping coffee,
from my balcony.
He pauses there daily,
and looks up at me.

He sports a red t-shirt
when it's a warm day.
When cool out, a hoody
that's red all the way.

He rides a red scooter
all over the place,
as free as a songbird,
the wind in his face.

If I could be fifteen
all over again,
I'd love to know him
at least as a friend.

If he were only legal
and leaned a bit gay,
I'd try to seduce him
every which way.

A bird out of reach,
and not mine to win,
he remains a fantasy,
my cardinal sin.

~g

YOU MAY NOW HIDE THE BRIDE

I'm covertly in love with someone,
who prefers that no one else know.
When I call him on his iPhone,
a faceless icon appears. It's so.

I'm forbidden to be on his Facebook,
for all his friends and family to see.
How could he explain my comments,
and justify what he is to me.

We've lived two lives for years now.
Outside we are simply good friends.
But inside, in private, we're lovers,
burning with passion that never ends.

Now he's talking rings and marriage,
but demands that I must first agree
to keep the news of husband and
husband, between us for eternity.

~g

CANDY MAN

Another gray, rainy day,
I'm watching TV in bed.
Nibbling nutty chocolates.
Should be writing instead.
I'm truly a manly writer.
One look and you'd agree.
But somehow soaps and
bonbons tend to bring out
the woman in me.

~g

BOY NEXT DOOR

There he is, Mr. Handsome,
always sporting a big smile.
He tends to stay inside a lot.
Think I'll gaze at him awhile.

Smooth, tan, and shirtless,
blue jeans and girlish stride.
Sets a stool over by the tree.
Looks my way. I do not hide.

Perhaps he wishes I join him.
Perhaps he longs for a friend.
Perhaps the boy has a hunger,
for a man with time to spend.

Unshaven and not showered,
scruffy, my hair's a hot mess.
Opportunity's knocking loudly.
Timing sucks, I must confess.

I want to engage him in story,
leave him eager, craving more.
Maybe tomorrow I'll be ready
to meet the boy next door.

~g

GOTH BOY

27

After saying goodbye, I came home
braced to accept being without you.
Instead, I found you still here: your
black T-shirt crumpled by the door,
glittery bracelet on the nightstand,
half full cigarette box on the floor.

All signs you were not just a dream,
memories of you I could still touch,
smell, and taste, that if I kept, you
might return another day to claim.
But, knowing better, I collected and
placed it all in a small white box.

I didn't want to let go of the package
as the postman took it from my hand.
I couldn't bear to see it go, having
to say goodbye to you all over again.
Though it was clear the day we met,
your spiked velvet collar had no leash.

~g

TUESDAY MORNING COMING DOWN

It's 8 AM Tuesday morning
and still no word from Tim.
I'm just sitting here sighing,
thinking thoughts of him.

I want so much to text him,
but don't know what to say.
A tear just hit my iPhone.
I'm feeling so vulnerably gay.

~g

THE PRINCE OF NAILS
(A Spoof of Genderous Proportions)

The prince had his nails did,
royally chillaxin' in a chair.
A manicure fit for a king,
or, perhaps a queen, but
girl, we'll not go there.

Young damsels heave deep
sighs at even the mere tho't:
not of bedding his highness,
but of his radiant beauty,
natural, not store bought.

"Mirror, mirror, on the wall,
why are we not as fair as he?"
Because he's the fairest of all,
you foolish maids, and your
Prince Charming he'll never be.

~g

CUDDLE BUDDY

Is it asking much,
for a little touch,
to be wrapped in
warm embrace,

To hold me tight
all thru the night,
as the moonlight
kisses my face,

No sticky strings,
or golden rings,
no making the
waters muddy,

No more pretend,
just a good friend,
to come be my
cuddle buddy?

~g

SUBTLE SEXUALITY

I don't wish to be one of *them*.
I just want to be loved as me.
I'd rather not be a social freak.
I just want to live hate free.

I don't march in Pride parades,
or wave a rainbow flag.
I don't stick it in their face that
I love guys, that I'm a fag.

I live my life quite normally.
I'm straight when on the streets.
But when at home, in privacy,
I'm so gay between the sheets.

~g

BAD BOY

You are such
a naughty
bad boy,
but in such
a pleasing
way.

Nothing short
of all boy,
so frisky
and
full of
play.

~g

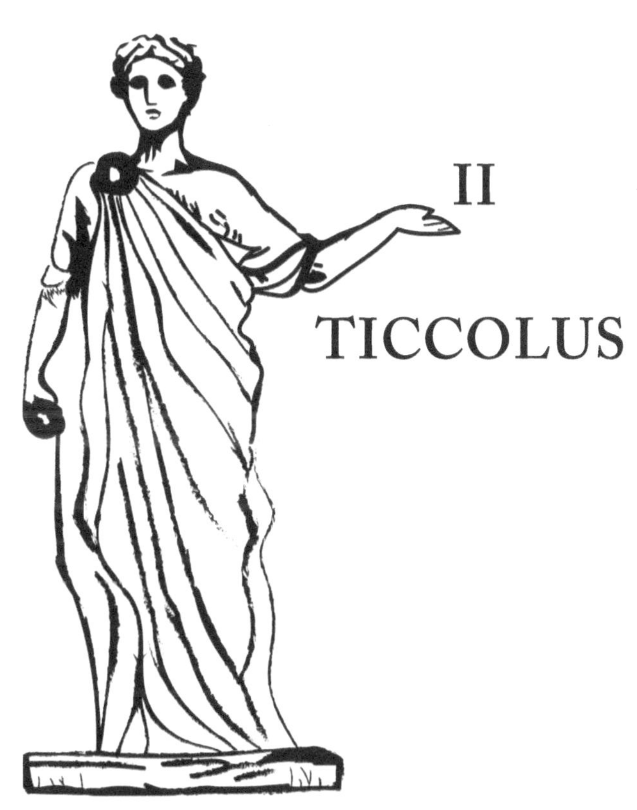

II

TICCOLUS

PLAY WITH ME

There's no
need to stay
with me.

Just come
have your way
with me.

Then we
might just let
things be,

Or perhaps
we'll become
good friends.

~g

KEEP IN TOUCH

A friend trusted me tonight.
I love it when that happens.
It opens so many new paths
and friendship possibilities.

It takes courage to shed one's
clothing, to reveal one's self
totally for the very first time,
nothing hidden, no mystery.

It takes trust to completely
relax, and to let the hands of
another rub oil everywhere,
and to massage everything.

A friend trusted me tonight.
I love it when that happens.

~g

CYBERLICIOUS

You're the
epitome of
eye candy,
so sumptuous
and sweet;
a cream-filled
Hostess Twinkie,
and good
enough to eat.

The hard in
my hard drive,
you press
all the right
keys;
a bold flirt
from a distance,
and, oh you're
such a tease.

So sensually
propitious,
someone who
I crave;
so sexually
auspicious,
my red hot
cyber knave.

~ g

PIC-PEC PONDERANCE

What's up with boys
online today?
Posing shirtless,
straight, bi, or gay?

Those oh so tight
washboard abs,
smooth, hard pecs
like iron slabs,

Low hung jeans like,
"I don't care,"
revealing sprigs of
"happy hair."

Might they just be
naughty flirts?
Or is it that they
own no shirts?

~g

EPIPHANY

Boom, boom, boom,
crowd-filled room;
color strobing lights,
people high as kites.

Sweaty shirtless guys,
promises and lies;
grinding ass 'n dongs,
booze, pills, 'n bongs.

Still a little hollow,
so again ya swallow;
feeling kinda rough,
still hangin' tough;

Your libido's zappin',
but it's gonna happen,
the price to be paid,
hoping to get laid.

Would of, should of,
perhaps ya could of;
tonight like the rest,
hoping for the best.

But ya cannot find,
what ya had in mind:
that fit hand in glove,
the right bud for love.

Stepping out the door,
tired, drunk, 'n sore;
sun kissin' ya face,
heart startin' to race.

Suddenly ya know,
a voice tells ya so;
more than a hot bod,
you're a child of God.

~g

PROUD CLOUD

Cotton candy
cloud cock,
erect against
the sky,
freely floating
fluffy fun,
looks anything
but shy.

Cotton candy
cloud cock,
soon no one
will see,
you fading,
going flaccid,
a playful
memory.

~g

GETTING IT ON

Wearing clothes is
much too restrictive.
Clothes can often be
rather vindictive.

Clothing inhibits
passion as it rises,
regardless of brand
names, or sizes.

Too many buttons,
snaps, and zippers,
turning lovers into
Jack the Rippers.

Wildly tearing,
tossing all aside,
yanking, pulling,
no need to hide.
Two exhausted,
determined guys,
breathing heavily,
going for the prize.

If everyone agreed
to not wear a stitch,
getting it on would
not be such a bitch.

~g

ALL OF YOU

I know you have a body
complete with every part:
two arms, two legs, a torso,
and a head to start.

Fingers made for touching
places longing for a touch.
Toes made for tickling,
and never kissed too much.

Ears to nibble and nuzzle,
to blow and whisper in.
Eyes to gaze in deeply
that reveal the soul within.

Lips full 'n soft for kissing,
so great for making love.
Tongue for licking all over,
until I scream "Enough!"

 And, oh, those special parts,
but need I be so blunt?
I lust for what's behind you,
and hanging in the front.

~g

HANGING OUT

There's quite a difference
between yours and mine,
not only in size, but
how artful and fine.

Mine's small and shriveled.
Yours, so smooth and long.
Mine's a grower not a shower.
Yours, my god, what a schlong!

With eyes straight forward,
peeking peripherally,
I can't help but admire
your fine junk as we pee.

~g

TRUE KENFESSION

Though I know that I can
never be Barbie,
I am so pleased we are
the best of friends;
enjoying our afternoons
walking the Mall,
scoping out the boys with
the nicest rear ends.

~g

MAY - DECEMBER

I want you to be expressive,
to say what's on your mind.
If I may get a word in edge-
wise, I'll reciprocate in kind.

You haven't any feelings
I have not felt before,
be they happiness, sorrow,
pleasure, pain, or more.

You haven't any thoughts
I have not thought before,
be they goody two shoes,
or wild ass raunch galore.

We both breathe the same air,
belch loud, and pass farts.
Though I'm clearly older,
we both sport the same parts.

We share the same senses,
hear, touch, taste, and smell,
although you more keenly,
me, admittedly not as well.

The life that we're living
is for us to share alone:
you younger, me not so, but
who'd have ever known?

Many ways we're different,
but mostly we're the same.
You're in your first quarter.
Me? I'm still in the game.

So much yet to teach you,
so many life firsts to share.
I promise not to laugh when
you find your first gray hair.

~g

DIVERSERY RHYME

Let's take a little time
with a nursery rhyme,
about these three
guys bathing.

It's innocent enough.
They're in the buff.
But to some it might
seem scathing.

Rub a dub, dub,
three men in one tub?
Now, what was that
author thinking?

Three strapping studs
grabbing at suds,
for a soap that's
always sinking.

"Oh, that's not it,
you silly twit!
Here, let us help
and guide you."
Rub a tug, tug,
three men in the tub,
having BIG fun in
a small venue.

~ g

WHAT? ME JEALOUS?

Oh, to be young, hung,
and beautiful,
so pleasing to the eyes.

Everyone wants a sniff,
a taste, and get
between your thighs.

You don't have to have
a brilliant mind, or
personality to get laid.

Only to be young, hung,
and beautiful.
Bitch, you got it made!

~g

ZACHANGEL

Spiritual, not necessarily holy,
heavenly creature from above,
frisky, mischievous, playful,
with a heart that's full of love.

~g

TABOO

In the quiet stillness
I would lay,
dreaming about how
we might play,

If I weren't as timid
as a mouse,
and got you to come
to my house.

We'd run our fingers
here and there,
tickle our bodies so
young and fair,

Clothed in darkness
in my room,
under the blankets
I assume,

Touching new places
we'd not been,
what comes natural,
far from sin.

How sweet the tho't
of me and you,
fucking young nymphs,
if not taboo.

~g

THE OLD HUNTER

If I were eighty years younger,
and had you in my sight,
I'd try my best to bag your ass,
and bang it day and night.

Oh, I'm a believer in romance,
but a patient man I'm not.
Near you I'd be a buck in heat,
because you're so damn hot.

I'd sniff you, lick you, eat you,
and mount you like a bull.
Do you 'til it made you scream,
'til you were pleasure full.

If I were eighty years younger,
and had you in my sight,
I'd try my best to bag your ass,
and bang it day and night.

~g

NAKED THOUGHTS

Thoughts of you stir in my head
not asleep, yet barely awake.
What on earth are you doing here?
I'm naked for heaven's sake!

Nakedness is as nakedness does,
and as one might suspect,
thinking of you being naked too,
gets me standing quite erect.

Have you naked thoughts of me?
How I wish that it were true.
Until such time that we hook up,
naked thoughts will have to do.

~g

TOYING WITH IT

One last time,
I'm sending
some rhyme,
on how you
might spend
your last days.

Like,

Looking about,
whipping it out,
beating
boredom in
pleasurable
ways.

Make it stand
in your hand,
then start it
in motion:
up and down,
up and down.

Don't be afraid,
you'll get paid,
even if you
get caught
wildly going
to town.

Just smile with
great pride.
You've nothing
to hide.
Give them a
memorable
show.

Now invite
them to try,
soon they'll
know why
it's such fun
playing with a
yo-yo.

~g

SECRET PLACE

There's a place
that we can go.
It's only for us,
no one can know.

There we undress,
get totally bare,
lay gently back,
abandon all care.

A touch, a kiss,
spirits set free.
I pleasure you,
you pleasure me.

There are no ties,
no guilt to erase,
just hot sex in
our secret place.

~g

THERE

To the light of a
million twinkling stars,
beneath the silhouettes
of tall coconut palms,
upon a sun-faded
Aztec cotton sheet,
spread across the
warm beach sands,
pouring sweat
with the least
little motion
in the humid tropical
night air,
cooled by occasional
splashes of breeze,
lying bare before God
and the Universe,
our bodies pounding
in the darkness
to the hypnotic rhythm
of ocean surf,
making love until the
coming of dawn.

~g

III

AROUSUS

A GUY THING

Gazing in your
eyes,
passion starts
to rise,
which comes as
no surprise,
with your
hand between
my thighs.

Don't you think
it wise,
we give our love
disguise,
tell friends
and family
lies,
seeing we both
are guys?

~g

NOCTURNAL ADMISSION

Last night,
asleep, and
totally bare,
I made love
to a boy who
wasn't there.

I hope he's
not there
again tonight,
kissing me,
touching me,
feeling so right.

~g

FAIRY JUICE

Ah, the wind beneath my wings,
cooling my fairy armpit things.
Fairy pheromones wafting free.
Come fairy lovers, flit with me.

Flitter, flitter, flutter, flutter,
fairy dust and peanut butter.
I wish I may, I wish I might
be making fairy love tonight.

Blow wind, blow. Lift me higher.
Waft my scent. Ignite a fire.
This horny fairy is on the loose,
thirsting for some fairy juice.

~g

UNTOLD TALE

I wrote a tale of
two lovers today,
in a poem that
no one will see.
Because
one just might be
you, let's say,
and the other just
might be me.

Once upon a time,
not so long ago,
in a mystical,
magical land,
they
two did meet,
their lust did grow,
and a wonderful
story began.

They rendezvoused
in a secret place,
under the stars
out in the wood.
First
once, then twice,
then upped the pace,
finding it harder
to be good.

A look, a laugh,
a poke, a touch,
closer and closer
grew their bond,
'til
soon both knew
without a doubt,
they both grew
more than fond.

But rules and roles
hung in their way,
so, neither dared
make the move,
'til
urges so strong,
came into play,
pulling them deeper
into the groove.

One starlit night,
the mood just right,
before Nature, and
in Nature's own,
clutching
so tight, they came
once, then twice,
more intensely than
either had known.

I wrote a tale of
two lovers today,
in a poem that
no one will see.
Because
one just might be
you, let's say,
and the other just
might be me.

~g

UNSPOKEN INTENTION

I want to have you naked
next to me in my bed.
Nothing is more truthful,
regardless what I've said.

Like,

How I'd love to meet you
out somewhere for a drink,
spend lots of time talking
to discover how you think.

How I love your writing,
the art that's in your mind,
how special you are to me,
a precious treasure find.

How I love your laughter,
or anything else instead, of
I want to have you naked
next to me in my bed.

~g

ALL SUMMER LONG

It was my birthday
down in Key West
out at a bar alone.
Feeling sad, downed
a few beers, when
I heard my phone.

Hi, it's me, Scotty!
Yes, it's been long.
Parents are away to
Miami a few days,
hope calling you
isn't wrong.

I'm tired of clubs.
Just watching TV
in just my briefs.
Let's hang out,
and cuddle to
Sex in the City.

Still to this day
I thank God above,
for Scotty,
and his sweet
summer long
love.

~g

SUMMER REFLECTION

Not too buff,
a hint of tough,
a beautifully rough
Adonis.

Slight detection
of deep reflection,
summer's benediction
upon us.

He had a blast,
the days now past,
wishing they could last
forever.

Getting laid,
here in the shade?
No, but yes, he made the
endeavor.

Another year,
he will return to the pier,
yes, he'll still be queer,
but older.

Having fun,
worshipping the sun,
hoping to fuck someone,
now bolder.

~g

STRAWBERRY FEELS FOREVER

Strawberry shortcake,
strawberry wine,
strawberry lubricant,
feeling berry fine.

Let me take you down,
you know the deal:
to strawberry feels.
This offer is real.

Nothing

to get hung about, so
no need to be hung.
Just "Yes, I want to,
and no, I'm not too
young."

~g

SOCIETUS INTERRUPTUS

Here we are.
Me looking at you,
you looking at me;
both sensing an
unmistakable attraction
one animal in heat has
for another.

I'm totally fighting
back the urge to
come sniff you.
Your posture betrays
your desire to
be mounted.
But we politely
maintain distance,
limiting courtship
to no more than
seductive, playful
glances.

Yet, through the façade,
primal urges churn
deeply within,
causing a
growing bulge in one's
Calvin Klein's,
and a wetness
one hopes the Armani's
don't reveal.

The feeling's hot,
the moment's so right,
but the timing's all
fucking wrong.

Caught in the midst
of the nine-to-five
corporate frenzy,
we've become slaves
to the clock.
In times past,
I would've taken you
right here, right now.

But, after all,
are we not
sophisticated,
civilized creatures,
long removed
from the
wild?

~g

RAINBOW BOYS

Rainbow boys
reach for toys
when life
becomes a bore.

Oh what joy
they employ,
fresh from the
porno store.

But,

After whipping,
dildo dipping,
they hunger
something more.

A kiss, a hug,
a snuggle bug,
it's love they
most long for.

~g

SUGAR PLUMS

Late one night,
fast asleep
in bed,
came visions
of
sugar plums
dancing
in my head.

Opening my
eyes I could
not see,
because
my
lover's balls
were tea
bagging me.

~g

ON THE QT

I thank God for my
quality time buddy,
who inspires me to
live life and let go.

Teaching me to be
less a fuddy-duddy,
to have raucous fun,
but on the down low.

Just thinking of him
turns my face ruddy:
a scandalous secret
no one can know.

~g

OLD ROOSTER'S TALE

One day the gate was left open,
the old rooster decided to flee.
For the very first time in his life,
he knew how it felt to be free.

He could go where he wanted,
no old hen to hold him back;
explore beyond the barnyard,
the depths of his soul, in fact.

For years he searched answers,
so much he had longed to know:
what a rooster was all about,
what pushed his buttons to crow.

Found he preferred young cocks.
He never loved old hens at all.
Clucking destroyed his libido.
Young cocks made him stand tall.

He met a young strapping rooster.
Thought it time they settled down.
At first, marriage was like heaven.
Things soured, soon turned around.

The crowing of the young rooster,
became cluck-clucks of an old hen.
"Be still. Go to sleep. Just roll over.
Not now, I've a headache again."

All he was mounting was tension.
His very roosterhood was at stake.
Day after day with no satisfaction.
How much more could he take?

Once a rooster, always a rooster:
born to jump it, hump it, and crow.
With an old hen, or a young rooster,
old roosters don't like to hear "No."

~g

SMÖRGÅSBORD

I'm afraid you cannot provide
all the nutrition I need.
I require more than one course
upon which to feed.

You've been the best main dish.
Oh yes, this is true.
But I'm hungry for side dishes,
and one just won't do.

No one could ever pleasure me
in ways that you can.
There's no substituting that dish.
For sex, you're the man.

Then there's the intellectual side.
My brain needs sex too.
I crave stimulating conversation.
That simply is not you.

When it comes to my spirituality,
I'm too weak to shout.
It's past time I had a soothsayer,
some spiritual "take-out."

My creative child's been starving
from the lack of a muse.
I need to find that someone who
naturally lights my fuse.

And then there's the dessert dish:
a personal soul mate,
one to share a deep affinity.
So long I've had to wait.

This is what I need to feed me
body, mind, and soul:
a smorgasbord of many friends,
perhaps, throw in a roll.

~g

BOYS OF SUMMER RISING

Knaves 'n waves 'n salty suds,
sunshine glistening on your buds,
wet, revealing swimming duds.
Tame those thoughts for now.

Wild, matted, windblown hair,
the smell of ocean in the air,
playing all day without a care.
Teasing comes so freely.

Tossing a football hand to hand,
with lots of tackling in the sand,
the body contact feels so grand.
Time will come for scoring.

Running, diving in headfirst,
sand in cracks feels the worst.
Frolicking naked builds a thirst.
It's five o'clock somewhere.

Drying off in nature's own,
how manly some have grown.
It's nice to see you're not alone.
Beer cans spurt in celebration.

Now with towels loosely hung,
sipping suds, the night is young.
One by one the empties flung,
as the need for sex keeps rising.

~g

HOOK UP

Twinkie, twinkie,
little porn star,
may I take you
from this bar?

Both above the
world so high.
First day light
is drawing nigh.

We'll sleep thru
the morning sun,
after wild ass,
naked fun.

Twinkie, twinkie,
little porn star,
I'm so pleased to
see you in my car.

~g

HEART ON

I never know
what to do
when we're
together.

I miss you
something
fierce when
we're apart.

I look for
signs you
keep well
hidden,

in your
boxers,
and in
your heart.

~g

COMPLETE

When holding your hand
I feel safe.
When lying beside you
I am home.

It's never been a matter of
who's stronger,
smarter, or who's cock
is longer.

Being together with you
I feel whole.
Being together with you
I am complete.

~g

CYBER GAY

Eating leftover home fries
right out of the pan,
scratching his package
with the other hand.

What else has he to do
so early in the morn,
other than jerking off
to some cyber porn?

Two hours before school,
and he's home alone,
strutting about the house,
dialing on his phone.

Hey Tim, get on Skype;
make it kind of quick.
I'm feeling very horny now,
stroking on my dick.

Fifteen miles out of town
somewhere on a farm,
Tim strips down quickly,
resets his alarm.

They meet on video chat,
like they often do,
fondling their phalluses,
ready to cyber screw.

I love your cock, Brent.
I want it in my ass.
I want you so bad, Tim,
so, someday after class?

Later I've marching band;
perhaps better if tonight?
Oh yeah, most definitely.
I bet it's nice 'n tight.

You still dating Mary Ann?
She has awesome breasts.
How's thing with your girl?
She gets me hot, then jets.

Doesn't have your cute ass,
nice balls, or sweet cock.
Touching her I think of you,
then whack off in a sock.

Oh God, I'm coming! You
did it again, you fool!
Me too! We'd better go, or
we'll be late for school.

Brent showers and dresses.
Tim takes time to snooze;
When not in public, cyber
gay is what they choose.

~g

YOUR PAGE OR MINE?

Cheap brandy in my coffee,
Cardbordeaux by the glass.
I spend days writing poetry,
with no depth, so little class.

Many missed opportunities,
chances I've readily blown.
I pen of loves most coveted,
of loves I've not yet known.

I write about more orgasms,
than will ever grace my bed.
The greatest of sexual trysts,
are the ones still in my head.

Many may think me a loner,
though I'm rarely ever alone.
With a pen and pad of paper,
I've always someone to bone.

~g

MILKSHAKE MYTH

If I were good for weed,
no doubt I'd have
friends indeed.

Had I free, endless booze,
no doubt I'd be who
they'd choose.

Had my fridge a 30-pack,
they'd show and keep
coming back.

User friends? Nothing new.
It's all about what they
get from you.

Facing truth can be hard.
Milkshakes don't bring
boys to my yard.

~g

LICK-A-PIC

Check out my
washboard
tummy,
and tell me
it isn't
yummy.

The truth's in
black 'n
white.
These abs are
nice 'n
tight.

Too bad it's
only a
pic,
but go ahead,
give it a
lick.

~g

FIRST MOVE

I'm afraid to offer you pleasure,
though it's always on my mind,
to risk a friendship I treasure,
should you not be so inclined.

Each time that we're together,
I hope you'll smile and say,
"Tickle my ass with a feather?
What do you say we play?"

Nothing then, could stop me.
Nothing could get in the way,
of great sex, hot and steamy,
day, after night, after day.

~g

BLINDSIDED

He was crushed
when he
found out
he had
actually
been jilted.

Now he shoots
his load
into
a swath
of Northern
Quilted.

His love life
has taken
a sharp
turn
with little
emotion.

Nothing more
than a loose
clenched fist
and a few
squirts of some
lotion.

Not the eye!
Bet he
didn't
see
THAT one
coming.

~g

LION'S DEN

Come, Daniel,
to the lion's den.
Come, little cub.
Come anytime.
Come often.

Let me unleash
your wild side,
pet your mane,
stroke those
furry places,

Until you roar
with delight,
and purr like
a pleasured
pussy.

~g

IV

PHUCCUS ALREDIUS

A GAY THING

I'm gay.
You're gay.
Enough
with
formality.
Let's fuck.

~g

YOUNG STALLION

Some prefer a
Porsche.
Others prefer a
Corvette.
I prefer a young
stallion,
ridden hard,
and
put away
wet.

~g

MOUNT 'N TOP

My submission?
Contemplation?
Yield myself
to penetration?

For you, I'd
have to say yes.
It'd please me,
I must confess.

Have you bang
against my thighs,
feel your body
fall and rise,

To watch your
eyes in ecstasy,
mouth parting as
you come in me.

Discomfort? No.
It'd be a pleasure
to offer up my
hidden treasure.

~g

NIGHT CAP

Stirring,
restless,
somewhere,
between love
and alone.

Slouching,
yawning,
staring,
in darkness
by the phone.

Scratching,
sighing,
sipping,
Sambuca
from a glass.

Inching,
rising,
throbbing,
cock crowing
for some ass.

~ g

PRETZEL

I love when we
play pretzel,
licking those
hot, salty spots
with our tongues,

How your legs
climb toward
the ceiling,
on a ladder that
has no rungs.

~g

TOUCH

Brush me
  publicly here,
  so privately there.

Caress me
  manly here,
  so boyishly there.

Squeeze me
  tightly here,
  so loosely there.

Rub me
  vigorously here,
  so gently there.

Stroke me
  roughly here
  so softly there.

Explore me
  wildly here,
  so tamely there.

Ravage me
  with your touch!
  Is that asking
  for too much?

~g

THIS BUD'S FOR YOU

I really don't know what
I would ever do,
if the day came when I
no longer had you;
you, breathing in my face
so close to my head,
you, sleeping like an angel
naked in my bed,
cuddling me like a pretzel
nice 'n buttery hot,
sweet, salty, 'n ready to
give it all you've got,
joyful in the thick times,
also in the lean,
caring for 'n doing for me,
never being mean,
making mundane moments
special in my life --
my best friend,
my fuck buddy,
my forever "wife."

~g

PLUGGING THE GAP

He was absolutely
adorable with his
devilish innocence,
frosted spiked hair,
diamond pierced ear,
dreamy baby blues,
perfect bubble butt
nicely wrapped in
Calvin Klein undies
in his Express jeans,
Abercrombie Boy abs
beneath his Hollister T,
Hot Topic collar with
matching glitter band,
looking at me with
that coy *fuck me* smile.

So, I did.

One by one I peeled
off the brand names,
strewing them like
rags about the room,
leaving him only in
his Adonis nakedness.
Hot with passion, and
driven by animal lust,
I was ripe for a night
of ravaging and being
ravaged, but—oh no—
it ended all too soon.
There was nothing
designer about his sex.
He came quickly,
rolled over, and invited
me to finish.

So, I did.

~g

LUST HURTS

One-night stand,
hot temptation,
  use me
  for your
masturbation.

Hollow whispers,
loveless pleasure,
  lick me,
  eat me,
take my treasure.

Promises spoken
soon forgotten.
  See me?
  Call me?
Truth is rotten.

~g

MARTI GRAS
MIDNIGHT PLOWED BOY

I see he joined another table
with a man in a cowboy hat.
He offers the stranger a beer.
They strike up a friendly chat.

I watch them from a distance
to see where it all might lead.
Is my fine, young stallion
hankering to be *his* steed?

I go cool off for ten, or so,
then return to claim my place.
Both are nowhere in sight now.
My heart speeds up its pace.

Two beers left on the table,
neither of the two in sight.
Perhaps a mere coincidence.
Perhaps what I fear is right.

I dash off to the Men's Room,
where guys go for a quick lay.
I'm shocked to find it locked.
No, it can't be them. No way.

I return every few minutes,
jiggle the handle on the door,
praying that he's not in there,
go check out front once more.

Pounding down my cocktail,
I try the bathroom door again.
This time it finally opens up,
but there's no one in it then.

I go back up front to look for
what I hope I will not find.
But goddamn it, there he is.
The image blows my mind!

He's groping the Cowboy,
deep throat kissing heavily.
A drunken fool lost in lust,
not caring who could see.

Had they fucked in the head?
The possibility's very strong.
How could this night of fun
have so suddenly gone wrong?

His party beads are missing,
and so is his costume hat.
His clothes are all disheveled.
He's no clue where he's at.

Swears that nothing happened.
Says he can't recall a thing.
But when I asked the cowboy,
he had a different song to sing.

~g

VERY SEXUAL, A LITTLE CORNY

I got up to write a poem today,
dawn is barely breaking.
Didn't sleep a wink last night,
now my head is aching.

I suppose I'll take two aspirin,
to help my brandy coffee,
and take my mind off the pain,
by sucking English toffee.

Writing poetry's much like sex:
eventually it will come.
Sometimes the wait is longer,
when I can't get some.

If I'd a sweet thing in my bed,
hell no, I'd not be writing.
But rather, I'd be sucking on him,
licking hard, and biting.

Now I'm feeling wide awake,
no pain, and a little horny.
I believe I've a poem in mind:
very sexual, a little corny.

~g

LITTLE RAINBOW PONY

Oh my god, girl!
What are you doing here?
Oh my god, girl!
You knew I was queer.

Oh my god, girl!
I'm bare ass naked, too!
Oh my god, girl!
What on earth did we do?

Oh my god, girl!
I don't remember a thing!
Oh my god, girl, I
OD'd on Singapore Sling!

Oh my god, girl!
My lover can't find out!
Oh my god girl!
He'd kick my young ass out!

Oh my god, girl!
You're giving me some wood!
Oh my god, girl!
It's starting to feel good!

Oh my god, girl!
Okay, I'll just shut up.
Ride this rainbow pony!
You go girl! Giddy up!

~g

LITTLE CURLIES

Here, there, and
everywhere,
on the bathroom sink,
the rim of
the toilet,
definitely yours,
I think.

Here, there, and
everywhere,
on a shower tile,
hiding in
the loofa,
and on a bar
of Dial.

Here, there, and
everywhere,
on the satin sheet,
on the kitchen
table,
now wasn't
that a treat!

Here, there, and
everywhere,
after going south,
my favorite place
for finding them
is hiding in
my mouth.

~g

INTRO TO MÉNAGE A TROIS

He called me on the
phone one night,
then came knocking
at my door.
We drank,
we laughed,
and
fooled around.
I knew he'd be
back for more.

The next time he
brought along
a she to join in
the sport.
We drank,
we laughed,
and
fooled around.
Though strange, I
did consort.

He with me,
me with she,
he and she both
watching me.
We kissed,
we fondled,
we got
major laid,
now easy as
one, two, three.

~g

INDIRECTLY SPEAKING

I wrote a naughty poem today
about some very naughty things:
what we like to do in private
with leather 'n hand cuff rings,

Cool Whip, Hershey's syrup,
hot, sweet desserts that delight,
whipping it all up in a lather,
licking it all off after we fight.

But I didn't divulge just who.
No, that would be crazy to do.
How we pleasure one another
remains between me and you.

I wrote a naughty poem today
about two very naughty boys,
the games they play together,
with whips 'n chains 'n toys.

~g

I'M TOTALLY INTO YOU

Your lips:
      the fullness of them,
      the feel of them,
      the taste of them.

Your pits:
      the smell of them,
      the feel of them,
      the taste of them.

Your cock:
      the smell of it,
      the feel of it,
      the taste of it.

Your ass:
      the smell of it.
      the feel of it.
      the taste of it.

I'm so totally into you.

~g

HOT PLATE SPECIAL

After the day was done
at the setting of the sun,
dining out seemed right,
on such a special night.

We uncorked some wine,
'til we were feeling fine.
Soon the fire did ignite,
and our jeans grew tight.

So,

We let our server know
that we decided on "to go."
Entrees cooled in the box as
we fed on hot, young cocks.

~g

HEAD TO THE LEFT AND COUGH

We're both adults, so
what can be wrong
with us having
a little fun?

I knew once we met,
it wouldn't take long
for lust to rise
like the sun.

Believe it or not,
I'm getting so hot,
to a degree I
cannot stand.

What do you say
you play doctor,
and cool my fever
with your hand.

~g

FREAKY GEEK

I'm sitting at home
with nothing to do,
looking at porn and
drinking beer.

If only there were a
horny young nerd
into role playing
with me here.

No complications,
no strings attached,
just pleasure for
pleasure's sake.

A discreet fuck bud
from time to time,
who likes to give as
well as take.

Where for art thou
freaky geek boy?
Daddy's waiting,
patiently.

Rubbing one off
just thinking about
how hot a nerdy
young ass might be.

~g

FOUR LEAF CLOVER

Landed ass first
on the floor
when I went
to roll over.

Must've gotten
drunk, naked,
and decided
to sleep over.

Three other
bare bods in
bed. Did we?
Over 'n over?

God, I need
some aspirin.
Feel like I was
beaten all over.

Can't complain.
There's no getting
luckier than a
four-leaf clover.

~g

CREAM OF MUSHROOM

In the forest
we go walking.
Holding hands,
we stop talking.

Pressed against
an old oak tree,
I fondle you,
you fondle me.

Shrooms growing
in the woods.
We're groping at
each other's goods.

Fresh produce,
not from cans,
wearing nothing
but our tans,

We stir and stir
the savory pot.
Lick it, taste it,
until it's hot.

No mistaking
when it's ready:
rich and frothy,
thick and heady.

Soup's on!

~g

BRAVISSIMO!

The house lights
dim to darkness
as the second violin
slowly makes his way
center stage
with poise
and purpose.
Nervously
inching closer
to his seat
he cradles the
instrument he's
longed to play
with another for
so long.

Voices of guilt
in his head
grow louder

with each step,
demanding
the music stop,
before it begins.
But the desire
to touch, to play,
his instrument
with another
grows increasingly
stronger,
soon melting
his inhibitions,
and fears.

He sits erect with
his instrument
resting against
his thighs as
the first violin

confidently
takes his seat,
their legs
rubbing gently
together,
as the orchestra
welcomes
its maestro.

With one
Masterful stroke,
he commands
the moment.
Raising
his wand,
their eyes
eagerly awaiting,
the music begins.

The maestro leads.
The young violinists
submissively follow.
A symphony of
musical pleasure,
pours freely
as never imagined.
And, at the
Maestro's lead,
they crescendo
so wonderfully,
so powerfully,
so satisfyingly.

~g

COCK-A-DOODLE-DOO

One young cock keeps
me up all night,
crowing his heart out
randomly;
one of a band of
young roosters
that roam around
aimlessly.

Another young cock
is now restless,
rising with passion,
playfully;
one of a band of
young suitors,
who seek a safe
place to be.

Key West has many
young roosters,
all crowing at night
for some ass;
some ignored in
the distance,
others getting laid
smoking grass.

~g

BACK SCRATCHERS

My roommate has a medical condition
that prevents him from ever driving.
I taxi him to work and back each day,
because it's how we're both surviving.

In these tough times of economic woes
doing favors has to come with a price.
When I said mine was gas, grass, or ass,
he just laughed at me and said, "Nice."

I scratch his back and he scratches mine,
both literally and figuratively speaking.
No money, no pot, he gives all he's got,
on a bed that never stops squeaking.

~g

BACK DOOR GENIE

On the shore
a turning tide
reveals a lamp
beneath
the sand.

In my reach,
there
on the beach,
I take it
in my hand.

Rubbing it
thrice, a
blinding light
takes me to a
magic land.

"What's your
pleasure? Sex,
or treasure?
Please, master,
understand.

Before you ask,
be at task.
You've a
bottom at
your command."

~g

AND THEN SOME

Stunning, alluring,
so sexually arousing,
seeing you.

Touching, hugging,
so warmly inviting,
feeling you.

Sniffing, inhaling,
so musky fragrant,
smelling you.

Kissing, licking,
so sinfully delicious,
tasting you.

Moaning, groaning,
so animally primal,
hearing you.

Desiring, wishing,
five more senses for
enjoying you.

~g

TWINKIE SHOTS

Tempt 'n tease,
tickle 'n touch,
twist 'n turn,
but
not too rough.
Then,
slurp until
you get
your fill
of
sweet cream
shots
of
Twinkie.

~g

PIROUETTE PROPOSITION

Sir, might there be a
possibility,
a young dancer with
agility,
limber, loose, and
bendable,
all positions freely
rend-able,
be this night wined,
dined, and bedded,
forever after which
indebted,
to explore nuances in
pleasure,
beyond the wildest
measure,
and
with sexual currency
repay
with all the passion of
ballet?

Sir, might there be?

~g

HANGOVER HORNIES

Hottie boy, Zachary jock,
tho't he could party 'n rock.
As the beers slammed down,
the silly clown,
got drunker on beer, after
beer, after bock.

Zachie says:

"Whatever man,
I drink what I can,
from dusk to dawn's early light.
I'm young. I'm hung.
Look out, here I come.
My orgasms are out of sight.

Yes, I'm the man.
Sex was my plan,
but I drank myself into a stupor.
I got high as a kite,
tho' the mood was so right,
my limp dick was a party pooper.

Now sick as a dog,
my tool's hard as a log,
what the fuck am I going to do?
I'll take a boy, or a girl,
I'm about to hurl, but
still horny for someone to screw."

~g

METROSEXUAL

I don't have a
preference.
I simply fuck
whatever
tickles my fancy,
and
fall in love with
whatever
catches my eye.

~g

EROTIC BREW

In some enchanted time
and place, with
moonlight shining on
our face, off
the path we start
to race, into
the deep, dark forest.

Soon we reach the
rendezvous, where
wooden kegs greet
me and you, they
brim with some
erotic brew. It's
time for us to party.

Way out there beneath
the stars, far
from the bustling noise
of cars, like
magic appears two
Mason jars, so we
tap those old kegs open.

Guzzling one, then two,
then three,
I look at you, you look
at me. Our

clothes fly off, we're
feeling free, only
half aware what's coming.

Dancing gaily among
the trees, we
tip our jars as oft
we please, 'til
we both fall down upon
our knees, and
almost die from laughing.

Spread out breathless on
the ground, so
drenched in sweat, we
fool around, 'til
lips meet lips, and then
we drown, one
so deeply in the other.

We make love all thru
the night, 'til
the gentle touch of
morning light, finds
us motionless, embraced
so tight --
two drunken lovers,
sleeping.

~ g

LOLLIPOP

When it comes
to eating
candy,
only one will do.
Because
nothing beats
the sweetness
in a
licky, sticky
evening
spent with you.

~g

ODE TO A TWINKIE

Twinkie, Twinkie,
cream-filled cake,
what a delicious
snack you make.

Off a scale of one
to ten is why I
lick you, eat you,
again, and again.

~g

HANDFUL

I've no where
more pressing
to be.
I've nothing
more important
to do,
than
to lay here
spooning
with my balls
snuggly cusped
by you.

~g

DEFINITION OF GREAT SEX

Um, me banging you,
of course, you
likewise banging me;

Cocks rock hard solid,
bumping, with
ball sacks swinging free;

Tonguing deeply with
our mouths, and
wanting to fuck fast;

Trying not to bust
a nut, to
make the moment last;

Tasting sweaty flesh,
musky sweet,
everywhere it pleases;

Probing butt holes with
our fingers,
anywhere else for teases;

Pounding it in and out,
in and out,
'til our Johnsons spasm;

Falling into a pleasure
coma, after
our mutual orgasm.

~g

MUTUAL CONJUGATION

Come:
  I come.
  You come.
  We both come.

Coming:
  I'm coming.
  You're coming.
  We're both coming.

Came:
  I came.
  You came.
  We both came.

~g

SHORT AND LONG OF IT

I wish I were a
succinct writer.
I wish I could be
more brief and
make my words
tighter.

Speaking of which,

If I had a girlfriend,
I'd delight her,
slap her ass and
slip inside her.
Hear her bitch I
should be wider.

Well, I don't.
And, I'm not.

Besides, it's guys
that make me hot.
With them I can
hit the spot.

Speaking of which,

If I had a boyfriend,
I would tease him,
slap his ass, grip
'n squeeze him.
hear him cry how
much I please him.

Well, I don't.
And, oh god, how
much I would.

I wish I were a
sensual writer.
I wish I could be
more descriptive and
make your briefs
tighter.

Well, I am.
And, hope I did.

~g

EPILOGUE

I first encountered the *force* as far back as grade school. About the time of puberty, I began to take notice of boys. I found myself gazing at them and wishing for opportunities to get near them. There was something special about them—not all, just a select few—those with the right mix of cuteness, personality, and an appealing form. Those boys cast a magical spell on me that would never be broken. But not to worry mom and dad. No way was I gay.

As a teenager, guys that radiated the *force* seemed to dominate my waking thoughts, and often made cameo appearances in my dreams. I fantasized having a sleepover with them, with us in my bed under the covers, in the dark, in only our underwear. But then, I'd quickly shake it off. Why? Because everyone knew only girls had sleepovers. Those boys each had one thing in common--like a musical tuning fork, they vibrated my strings— and vibrated them in a way that felt so, so good!

I was confused by the feelings, yet I welcomed
them. I wondered why I never experienced such
feelings being around girls, not even with the
cutest ones in school. But, hey—it was just a me
wanted to be like them thing. Still, no way was I
gay.

As a young man, I found it odd that there were
always cuter guys around to capture my attention
at any given time than there were cute girls.
My family moved a lot. Once arriving in a new
town, I would make an effort to scout out guys
that unmistakably possessed the *force*. Careful to
maintain a safe distance, I took pleasure in their
handsomeness, beauty, fine honed bodies. Oh,
how I would let my mind wander with thoughts
of what getting close to them--I mean real close-
-would be like. But, gay? Oh, come on. Really?
Don't be ridiculous. I don't think so. It was
obvious.

cont.

EPILOGUE CONT.

Gay guys were effeminate. I'm far from it. Gay guys don't simply walk--they sachet. Gay guys don't simply talk—they imitate the mannerisms of girls. And besides, gay guys dress way too nicely. I was none of those things. I was always a blue jean, pullover, sneakers kind of guy. I was on the soccer team. I was on the basketball team. I was in the Boy Scouts, for God's sake! So, you see? There's no way I could be gay.

Besides, gay guys go to sleazy bars and dance clubs to pick up other gay guys for nothing more than quick, cheap, lust-in-the-dust sex in darkened booths, in filthy men's rooms, in trashy alleyways. I could never do something like that; especially if it were with a boyfriend. My boyfriend would know without a doubt that I loved him, cherished him, and respected him way more than that. So, there you go. I can't be gay.

However, now I find myself very troubled and deeply frustrated most of the time, and I have no clue why. I've tried so hard to live according to established rules set by my family and society, but feel empty, unfulfilled, and so lonely. I know in my heart of hearts I need someone. I need to be in a relationship, a loving relationship, an intimate relationship; a relationship with someone who is adorable, has a warm personality, and of course, a hot body, and makes my strings vibrate! I need…I need…a boyfriend. Oh my God! What am I saying? Have I become gay? No, I don't think so. I'm just now realizing that I've always been.

"Surrender to the *force*, young Skywalker. Come. Come to the gay side!"

~ G. Tristan Tarot

ABOUT THE AUTHOR

 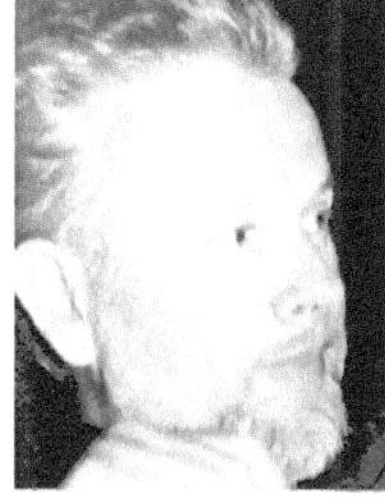 

Totally In   One Foot Out   Totally Out

G. Tristan Tarot is a freelance author and Adjunct Professor of English. He holds a graduate degree in writing from The Johns Hopkins University. He has enjoyed over fifteen years of teaching experience, following a split service military career in the U.S. Air Force and the U.S. Army. He has acquired an extensive firsthand knowledge on the wiles and ways of young adults. In many ways, he is still very much one himself.

Consider visiting the Orangenous Zone, www.gtristantarot.com, G.Tristan Tarot's personal website where the open-minded reader like yourself can experience fresh, juicy, poetry and verse written in good taste, and intended not only to quench the thirst of heart and mind, but also the libido. There you may read and follow Tarot's blog, find links to his works available for purchase, and links to promotional and YouTube videos. Whether your interest lies in adult short story, adult poetry, or milder sensual poetry, the Orangenous Zone has a little something to offer everyone.

You may also follow the author on:

Facebook: G. Tristan Tarot

Instagram: gtristantarot